Writing a Persuasive Essay

By

R.E. MYERS

COPYRIGHT © 2006 Mark Twain Media, Inc.

ISBN 1-58037-323-2

Printing No. CD-404051

Mark Twain Media, Inc., Publishers
Distributed by Carson-Dellosa Publishing Company, Inc.

Table of Contents

Introduction

This book has a sequencing of lessons that is meant to be followed from the first to the last. Thus, students are expected to engage in the activities of Lesson 1, "Directions for Writing a Persuasive Essay," and keep on going through the lessons in their numerical order until the last one, "Writing Your Persuasive Essay," is completed. Along the way, your students will encounter ideas about how a persuasive essay is conceived, constructed, and revised.

Some authorities feel that persuasive writing is important, not only because it requires disciplined thinking, but also because persuading others is something we do all of the time. They believe it is a good idea to teach young people how to write persuasively because writing forces the individual to put his/her thoughts in a form that is understandable to others; and, of course, writing can be revised, reviewed, and preserved. I agree.

As is the case in becoming proficient in literary endeavors, learning to write an essay means acquiring several discrete skills. By combining those skills, the student will be able to present an argument that should strike a reader as cogent and reasonable. The essay obviously won't convince every reader of the student's argument, but if well-done, the essay should give its audience a reason to consider the writer's opinion seriously.

That goal is the primary one that inspired the creation of *Writing a Persuasive Essay*. The lessons that follow were written in the hope that students will become better at arguing both in essays and in other forms of writing after having engaged in them. We know that certain instructional experiences have long-range consequences on young people. I sincerely hope that this book will have positive effects on your students both now and in the future.

Lesson 1: Directions for Writing a Persuasive Essay

TO THE TEACHER/PARENT: ABOUT THE LESSON

This first lesson is the foundation for the other lessons in this book. It is designed to be a source of information and guidance for your students. Students are invited to comment upon the eleven steps in writing the persuasive essay by making suggestions as to whether these should be extended or shortened.

Every authority regarding essay writing emphasizes that it derives from the personal viewpoint of the writer and thus can be distinguished from the article or treatise, both of which imply that the writer is objective and unbiased. The essay is an opinion piece.

Your students should have a copy of Lesson 1 and be able to refer to it when the time comes for them to write their essays.

As a pre-test activity to assess how much your students already know about persuasive essay writing, they should write a short essay persuading younger students to eat a balanced diet to maintain a healthy lifestyle. At the end of the book, students can revisit this topic by writing another essay. You and they can then determine how much the students have learned about persuasive essay writing by comparing the two essays.

Name: _____ Date: _____

Lesson 1: Directions for Writing a Persuasive Essay (cont.)

TO THE STUDENT

Except for letters and brief communications such as notes and memos, you are likely to write essays more often than any other kind of writing. One reason is that teachers in high school and college frequently have students write essays as assignments or for tests. The essay then, at least in school, is a form that you should want to master.

Of the various kinds of essays, the persuasive essay is the most powerful because it gives you the opportunity to convince someone of your belief or opinion about a topic. You not only present your viewpoint about the topic, but you back up your position with facts, examples, comparisons, quotations by authorities, and illustrations. Accordingly, the persuasive essay is a *reasoned* argument.

These are the steps you should take to write a persuasive essay:

1. **Choose a problem to write about.** Select a problem about which you feel strongly. Your thinking about the topic should be clear, not fuzzy.

2. **Write a definition of the principal terms regarding the problem.** By writing a definition of the terms, you can make clear to yourself and to your readers what exactly you are discussing.

3. **Keep your audience in mind.** Who will be the readers of your essay? What are they like?

4. **Summarize your position regarding the problem in a single sentence.** This is your thesis statement.

5. **Make an outline of your essay.** With your thesis statement as a guide, outline the main parts of your essay.

6. **Write a rough draft of your essay.** Express your ideas in sentences and paragraphs as indicated by your outline. Don't be too concerned with spelling, punctuation, or grammar at this stage. Leave plenty of space between lines for corrections.

Name: _____ Date: _____

Lesson 1: Directions for Writing a Persuasive Essay (cont.)

7. **Read your first draft over silently, and then read it aloud.** Make obvious corrections and rewrite awkward sentences. Put it aside and don't look at it for a few hours or a day.

8. **Make the corrections and changes that you see should be made.** Look for one kind of error or weakness at a time.

Here are the main areas in which possible errors or weaknesses might occur:

- **Mechanics:** Check your essay for errors in punctuation, spelling, sentence construction, and grammar.

- **Consistency:** Have you given enough details so a reader can follow the reasoning of your argument?

- **Development:** Are the main parts of the essay put together in a logical sequence? Does the material at the beginning grow as the essay develops?

- **Clarity:** Your thinking about the problem should be clear. Anyone who tries to persuade someone to share his or her opinion has a responsibility to examine that opinion closely. Ask yourself why you have that particular viewpoint.

- **Total effect:** Do you believe your readers will see, feel, and understand what you have written? If not, add or remove details so they will.

9. **Give the second draft to someone you respect, and ask for frank comments.**

10. **After the trial reader has read your essay critically, discuss it with him or her.** Make sure you understand any criticisms or suggestions.

11. **Rewrite your essay in light of your trial reader's critique.**

Lesson 1: Directions for Writing a Persuasive Essay (cont.)

Are there any steps you would add to the ones above? If so, what are they?

_____

_____

_____

_____

_____

_____

Would you eliminate any of the eleven steps? If so, which ones, and why would you skip them?

_____

_____

_____

_____

_____

_____

Lesson 1: Directions for Writing a Persuasive Essay (cont.)

These are the main features of a persuasive essay:

- **Purpose:** Your purpose in writing an essay is to persuade people concerning your viewpoint. This will more likely be successful if you have strong opinions about the topic.

- **Topic:** Your essay will succeed only if you can entice your readers to read it. An appealing topic with an intriguing title and a strong beginning will help to get the reader's attention. Be sure to limit its scope so you can do justice to the topic.

- **Audience:** Persuasion requires tact, careful use of language, a systematic marshaling of evidence, and an awareness of the characteristics of your audience.

- **Introductory statement:** At the beginning of the essay, you should clearly state the problem as you see it.

- **Support:** You must have enough evidence to support your viewpoint or argument. Anecdotes, comparisons, examples, and quotations by authorities are helpful in building your case. Facts used must be related directly to the argument put forth. You can make an effective argument by giving a series of facts, and then tying them together in a generalization.

- **Conclusion:** Your essay should end with a summing-up of your argument. You may also want to include a call to action in your concluding remarks.

Lesson 1: Directions for Writing a Persuasive Essay (cont.)

PRE-TEST ESSAY ACTIVITY

To determine how much you already know about persuasive essay writing, write a short essay (at least three paragraphs) in which you try to persuade younger students to eat a balanced diet in order to maintain a healthy lifestyle.

Remember to summarize your position with a thesis statement; support your position with facts, examples, anecdotes, and/or quotes; and restate your position in a conclusion.

_____

_____

_____

_____

_____

_____

_____

_____

_____

_____

_____

_____

_____

_____

Lesson 1: Directions for Writing a Persuasive Essay (cont.)

_____

_____

_____

_____

_____

_____

_____

_____

_____

_____

_____

_____

_____

_____

_____

_____

_____

_____

_____

_____

Lesson 2: Analyzing a Persuasive Essay

TO THE TEACHER/PARENT: ABOUT THE LESSON

The second lesson has your students taking a close look at a persuasive essay. As stated in the lesson, this is not the work of a professional writer. The student who wrote "Why We Are Rebelling" was fulfilling an assignment, and he was aware that elements such as examples, facts, anecdotes, and quotations by authorities should be included in his essay. Typically, the student's essay was probably too broad in scope, but he made it down-to-earth with his anecdotes. Whether the essay as such "connects" with your students is problematical; however, it is used as an example of a persuasive essay, not for its content, but for its form.

Why We Are Rebelling

statement of the problem

Why are more and more young people rebelling? Before answering this question, I'll try to define rebellion. Rebellion is open resistance to authority. It may be social, academic, parental, or any form of authority against which the individual can rebel. A rebellious youth can be called any number of things. Parents can call him a "bad boy" or her a "bad girl." Teachers can call the young person "incorrigible" or "insolent." Social workers might say he or she is "emotionally disturbed." And if the young person runs afoul of the law, he or she is classed as a "delinquent." But regardless of the words used, a young person is exhibiting behavior that is different from the norm and is disapproved of by an authority.

definition with the component parts

restatement of the definition

But why <u>do</u> young people rebel?

1st component: parental

Children need to feel loved. They need affection and a sense of belonging. When a young person is rejected by a parent, he or she may rebel in order to compensate for the loss of basic needs. The individual may feel dominated by one or both parents. The parent can become angry when the son or daughter talks back, fights with brothers and/or sisters, steals, drinks, or takes drugs. I might use myself as an example. Two of my close friends and I come from homes where one parent is an alcoholic. When we were younger, we would sneak out of the house day and night just to escape from the tense atmosphere. We would argue with our parents when they tried to discipline us or give us advice because, as one of my friends put it, "How can my father think he can tell me what to do when he's such a jerk himself?"

examples

anecdote

Lesson 2: Analyzing a Persuasive Essay (cont.)

2nd component: physiological

examples (generalizations)

anecdote

A young person may be rebellious because certain physiological needs are not being met. When I was in a third-grade class last fall as a volunteer, I found that children who are restless, fidgety, cranky, and uncooperative are often hungry, cold, ill, or even hard-of-hearing. In one case, the problem was quite serious. One boy continually created disturbances in the classroom. After lunch, he behaved himself for a while, but then he would run around the classroom, fight with other children, and sometimes even try to jump out of the window. Later on, they found that he had hypoglycemia, a condition causing a deficiency in blood sugar, and when the condition was arrested, the boy behaved normally.

3rd component: psychological

quote from an authority

summary statement

The famous psychologist Abraham Maslow believed that rebellion can occur from a lack of esteem, which he classified into two areas. "First the desire for strength, for achievement, for adequacy, for confidence in the face of the world, and for independence and freedom. Second, we have what we may call the desire for reputation or prestige (defining it as respect or esteem from other people), recognition, attention, importance, or appreciation." Maslow says that the lack of these needs being met may cause feelings of inferiority, weakness, or helplessness, and these feelings give rise to "either basic discouragement or else compensatory or neurotic trends." Young people need opportunities to express independence and freedom. They need to explore, to experiment, and to find out some things for themselves.

4th component: social

example

quote from an authority

A young person's peer group can play a great role in the person's desire for independence and freedom. Often what a person's friends are doing is counter to the beliefs and wishes of the parents, placing the person in an awkward position. If the pull to one side is much stronger than to the other, the person can be alienated from one of the two sides. This can cause rebellion. A.S. Neill felt that children should have freedom to follow their own interests. Parents may be part of what he called "the law of the crowd." They cling to old emotional values and are "afraid to give freedom to the young child because the parent fears that the young may indeed do all the things that the adult has wanted to do. The eternal impositions on children of adult conceptions and values is a great sin against childhood."

Lesson 2: Analyzing a Persuasive Essay (cont.)

summary statement

Thus, a young person may rebel from a lack of love and attention, a physiological need, a lack of esteem, or a lack of an opportunity to express independence and freedom. Or he may have lost respect for himself or others. There are many reasons why young people nowadays rebel against authority.

argument

call to action

For all of these reasons, I believe that society must do something to help young people who are trying to make their way in a troubled and troublesome world. A counselor should be assigned to every public school in the country, both elementary and secondary. There must be someone to whom the young people can go in order to get support and understanding. Society, if it is to actually solve these problems of defected and dejected youth, must address them directly—and soon. Our juvenile justice system is being overwhelmed.

Targeted Learner Responses: The student will identify the elements of a persuasive essay in an essay entitled "Why We Are Rebelling."

Name: _____ Date: _____

Lesson 2: Analyzing a Persuasive Essay (cont.)

TO THE STUDENT

Now that you have read what a persuasive essay is and how you can write one, it is probably a good idea for you to have an example of one. The essay that follows was written by a student and was not meant to be published. It has most of the elements necessary to make a persuasive essay effective. Read it over quickly once, and then read it again, carefully.

Why We Are Rebelling

Why are more and more young people rebelling? Before answering this question, I'll try to define rebellion. Rebellion is open resistance to authority. It may be social, academic, parental, or any form of authority against which the individual can rebel. A rebellious youth can be called any number of things. Parents can call him a "bad boy" or her a "bad girl." Teachers can call the young person "incorrigible" or "insolent." Social workers might say he or she is "emotionally disturbed." And if the young person runs afoul of the law, he or she is classed as a "delinquent." But regardless of the words used, a young person is exhibiting behavior that is different from the norm and is disapproved of by an authority.

But why <u>do</u> young people rebel?

Children need to feel loved. They need affection and a sense of belonging. When a young person is rejected by a parent, he or she may rebel in order to compensate for the loss of basic needs. The individual may feel dominated by one or both parents. The parent can become angry when the son or daughter talks back, fights with brothers and/or sisters, steals, drinks,

Lesson 2: Analyzing a Persuasive Essay (cont.)

or takes drugs. I might use myself as an example. Two of my close friends and I come from homes where one parent is an alcoholic. When we were younger, we would sneak out of the house day and night just to escape from the tense atmosphere. We would argue with our parents when they tried to discipline us or give us advice because, as one of my friends put it, "How can my father think he can tell me what to do when he's such a jerk himself?"

A young person may be rebellious because certain physiological needs are not being met. When I was in a third-grade class last fall as a volunteer, I found that children who are restless, fidgety, cranky, and uncooperative are often hungry, cold, ill, or even hard-of-hearing. In one case, the problem was quite serious. One boy continually created disturbances in the classroom. After lunch, he behaved himself for a while, but then he would run around the classroom, fight with other children, and sometimes even try to jump out the window. Later on, they found that he had hypoglycemia, a condition causing a deficiency in blood sugar, and when the condition was arrested, the boy behaved normally.

The famous psychologist Abraham Maslow believed that rebellion can occur from a lack of esteem, which he classified into two areas. "First the desire for strength, for achievement, for adequacy, for confidence in the face of the world, and for independence and freedom. Second, we have what we may call the desire for reputation or prestige (defining it as respect or esteem from other people), recognition, attention, importance, or appreciation." Maslow says that the lack of these needs being met may cause feelings of inferiority, weakness, or helplessness, and these feelings give rise to "either basic discouragement or else compensatory or neurotic trends." Young people need

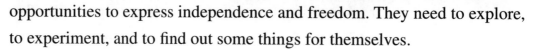

Lesson 2: Analyzing a Persuasive Essay (cont.)

opportunities to express independence and freedom. They need to explore, to experiment, and to find out some things for themselves.

A young person's peer group can play a great role in the person's desire for independence and freedom. Often what a person's friends are doing is counter to the beliefs and wishes of the parents, placing the person in an awkward position. If the pull to one side is much stronger than to the other, the person can be alienated from one of the two sides. This can cause rebellion. A.S. Neill felt that children should have freedom to follow their own interests. Parents may be part of what he called "the law of the crowd." They cling to old emotional values and are "afraid to give freedom to the young child because the parent fears that the young may indeed do all the things that the adult has wanted to do. The eternal impositions on children of adult conceptions and values is a great sin against childhood."

Thus, a young person may rebel from a lack of love and attention, a physiological need, a lack of esteem, or a lack of an opportunity to express independence and freedom. Or he may have lost respect for himself or others. There are many reasons why young people nowadays rebel against authority.

For all of these reasons, I believe that society must do something to help young people who are trying to make their way in a troubled and troublesome world. A counselor should be assigned to every public school in the country, both elementary and secondary. There must be someone to whom the young people can go in order to get support and understanding. Society, if it is to actually solve these problems of defected and dejected youth, must address them directly—and soon. Our juvenile justice system is being overwhelmed.

Now, in the left-hand margin, note the elements that the writer has used in making his statement. What evidence has been given to support the writer's position? Refer to the material in Lesson 1 before you make your notations.

Lesson 3: Choosing a Topic

TO THE TEACHER/PARENT: ABOUT THE LESSON

When your students have completed this lesson, they should be fully prepared to tackle the remaining lessons in the book. Getting a good idea of what they will write about is all-important. The topic chosen should be one that they care about, and formulating a thesis statement that expresses that concern is the key to writing an effective essay. The thesis statement is the most important part of the pre-writing activities that take place before the first draft is written. It controls and directs the essay.

EVALUATING STUDENT RESPONSES

Although we have given some examples of typical thesis statements and also offered one in the second lesson, you will want to go over the ones your students have formulated to see if they are manageable and in proper form. There could be some misunderstandings about the form of the thesis statement. At this stage, it should be a declarative sentence. Later on, it can be transformed into an imperative or interrogatory sentence. Make sure each student has narrowed the topic to a size to which he or she can do justice.

Name: _____ Date: _____

Lesson 3: Choosing a Topic (cont.)

TO THE STUDENT

Here are some categories of topics from which you can choose in preparing to write a persuasive essay:

- Social Problems
- Economic Problems
- Recreational Problems (including sports)
- Religious/Ethical Problems
- Intellectual/Educational Problems
- Problems or Issues in the Arts
- Communication Problems
- Transportation Problems
- Technological Problems
- Political Problems

A.   About which topic from the above list would you like to write?

_____

_____

B.   Give at least two reasons why you would like to write about that particular topic.

1. _____

_____

_____

2. _____

_____

_____

Name: _____ Date: _____

Lesson 3: Choosing a Topic (cont.)

Now that you have selected a subject that you care about, narrow it down so that you will be able to discuss it rather thoroughly. If you don't limit your subject to a reasonable size, you will have too much to cover in making a convincing argument. For example, instead of writing about the problem of homeless people in the country, you can write about the plight of the homeless in your own community and suggest something that can be done about it.

Write your subject again in the space below and put it in a thesis statement or proposition. These are the criteria for a thesis statement:

1. It should be a simple, declarative sentence.
2. It should be as concise and straightforward as possible.
3. It should indicate the writer's approach to the subject.
4. It sets limits on the subject.
5. It should reflect the writer's way of approaching a particular audience.

These are examples of typical thesis statements:

- Illegal immigrants are hurting our job market.
- Affordable housing is our greatest concern in this community, and we must do something about it now.
- The fashion in women's shoes goes from one extreme to another, which hurts both their feet and their pocketbooks.
- Steroids are a problem right here in our high school.

Write your thesis statement here:

_____

_____

_____

_____

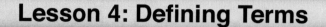

Lesson 4: Defining Terms

TO THE TEACHER/PARENT: ABOUT THE LESSON

As stated in the lesson, defining the most important terms of an essay can eliminate some of the misunderstandings that often occur when people argue. In itself, the definition is not a part of the argument, of course. The procedure recommended is quite thorough, but your students won't go wrong in following it if they are sincere in preparing to write a convincing essay.

EVALUATING STUDENT RESPONSES

If they follow the example given in the lesson, the definitions that your students write will propel them forward into the essay-writing mode. You probably won't get too many definitions from them that are as well-crafted as the one on rebellion, but it does present a good model for them to emulate.

FOLLOWING THROUGH

Your students might profit from examining a second example of a definition. This one, which was written when people in our country were concerned about loyalty in time of war, is briefer than the one on rebellion.

Loyalty

The idea of being loyal to someone, to an institution, to a country, or to a cause is an important one in our culture. A faithful friend is one who doesn't desert you. He or she can be depended upon to come to your aid or to defend you if it is necessary. Some people—politicians, soldiers, and many lovers among them—believe that loyalty is the most important virtue in human relationships. To these people, disloyalty or unfaithfulness is a disagreeable crime.

Name: _____ Date: _____

Lesson 4: Defining Terms (cont.)

TO THE STUDENT

When two people are discussing a topic, it is very important that they both have approximately the same understanding of the terms they are using, especially the terms that are basic to the topic. In that way, they can proceed with the discussion without being confounded by misinterpretations and misunderstandings. In the same way, in a debate or in a persuasive essay, it is critical to define the basic terms of the subject. You can go a long way in making sure that there is no misunderstanding of what you are proposing in a persuasive essay by following the directions below.

To understand a concept, especially a term used in writing about a topic, a definition is crucial for an understanding between the writer and the reader. It should include the distinguishing characteristics of the term and show how it is ordinarily used and understood.

DIRECTIONS

1. After picking a topic, you can get a better understanding of that topic and its ramifications by defining its central concept. In defining it, you set the limits and give the essential characteristics of the concept.

2. Read your definition and ask yourself if you have captured the basic idea of the concept. Do you get a sense of what it is when you use the term?

ELEMENTS OF A DEFINITION

Meaning: The commonly understood signification of the concept

Description: The basic characteristics of the term

Synonyms: The words that come closest in meaning to the concept

Antonyms: Words meaning the opposite of the concept; used for purposes of contrast or distinction

Examples: Sentences and phrases in which the concept occurs

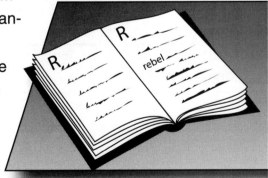

Name: _____ Date: _____

Lesson 4: Defining Terms (cont.)

DEFINITION

Rebellion

Rebellion can come in many forms. Basically, it is resistance to, or rejection of, authority. When we hear the word "rebel" these days, it usually refers to an individual whose behavior in some way runs counter to the authority of a parent, a school or other institution, or a country. Rebels are dissenters who disagree with the majority, the followers who obediently accept authority. The rebels we hear or read about are often guerrillas fighting against an established government or individuals acting out against the rules or norms of society. Rebellion also occurs naturally in the social and emotional development of an individual because it is the rejection of blind obedience. That is, at several points in a person's lifetime, it is normal to rebel in order to gain a healthy amount of independence. Refusing to eat your vegetables is a relatively mild form of rebellion.

As you can see, the writer of "Why We Are Rebelling" was able to spell out just what he meant by the term *rebellion*. Go through the same steps as he did and define the most important term dealing with the subject you have chosen. Most likely, it will be in your thesis statement.

_____

_____

_____

_____

_____

_____

Lesson 5: Writing a Trial Paragraph

TO THE TEACHER/PARENT: ABOUT THE LESSON

This lesson is meant to set up the one that follows it, namely, the gathering of information. By asking your students to write a paragraph about the topic they have chosen, we want them to see the necessity of obtaining further support for their argument. This is accomplished by bluntly asking them what else they need for a persuasive argument. Of course, many students are quite willing to write the one paragraph and let it go at that. The underlying idea of these lessons, however, is that to write an effective essay, the writer must do some thinking, some research, and some organizing. Persuasive essays are work. There's no getting around it.

EVALUATING STUDENT RESPONSES

To determine how your students are progressing toward the successful writing of a persuasive essay, you will have to scrutinize their efforts on this lesson. It is probably one of the more crucial lessons in the book because they will get a good idea of what their thinking is like concerning the topic they have chosen. Will their arguments hold water or just seem to be shallow opinions or rantings?

To be honest, experts in the field of writing have always expected too much of students when it comes to writing a paragraph. If you look at a paragraph at random in an article, story, or report, it usually doesn't have all of the elements that the experts would say it should have. For one thing, every paragraph in a well-written piece doesn't have a topic sentence and a summarizing statement. Far from it! Nevertheless, for the purposes of this lesson in this book, we are asking for both of those elements, knowing that the students' paragraphs in their essays won't generally be constructed as prescribed by the experts.

Name: _____ Date: _____

Lesson 5: Writing a Trial Paragraph (cont.)

TO THE STUDENT

1.   What is the topic for the essay you are to write? _____

_____

_____

2.   Write some remarks about your topic. _____

_____

_____

_____

_____

_____

3.   Now organize your remarks into a paragraph. Make sure it has a topic sentence and a summarizing statement. In this case, the topic sentence should also be the thesis statement of your essay. Use your own paper if you need more room.

Ideally, the paragraph should be organized in this way:

   a. Topic sentence
   b. Reasons for your position
   c. Supporting facts, examples, and anecdotes
   d. Generalization (summarizing statement)

_____

_____

_____

Name: _____ Date: _____

Lesson 5: Writing a Trial Paragraph (cont.)

_____

_____

_____

_____

_____

_____

_____

_____

_____

_____

_____

_____

_____

_____

_____

_____

Name: _____ Date: _____

Lesson 5: Writing a Trial Paragraph (cont.)

4.   Take a hard look at the paragraph you have just written. Does it make a convincing argument? Further support for your argument is undoubtedly needed because you have written only one paragraph. What will you need in order to present a strong argument? List the elements below that are needed and beside them note where you think you can obtain the information. For example, for obtaining authoritative information, you might write the names of people to interview and quote.

_____

_____

_____

_____

_____

_____

_____

_____

_____

_____

_____

_____

Lesson 6: Gathering Information and Using Facts

TO THE TEACHER/PARENT: ABOUT THE LESSON

Lesson 6 ("Gathering Information and Using Facts") should follow Lesson 5 ("Writing a Trial Paragraph") closely in time. Your students are to refer back to Lesson 5 for the elements that they thought should be added to their paragraphs in order to make their arguments complete. Then they are to think about where they will get the needed information. This is one of the crucial steps in writing an essay; that is, in order to write a convincing essay, your students will have to be able to back up their arguments.

Many students have written persuasive essays without offering sufficient support, hoping to get by with generalizations and ad hominem statements. Sometimes they are successful in concealing their lack of research, but more often their teachers (and others) see through the subterfuge. If they follow the precepts and dictates of these lessons, your students won't be able to fake it.

EVALUATING STUDENT RESPONSES

Among the sources for the information they need, your students may list the following:

- **Facts:** reference books, the Internet, periodicals, government documents, reports from industry, television, radio, friends and relatives

- **Examples:** personal experiences and the experiences of others, reference books, periodicals, television, radio, the Internet

- **Quotations:** reference books, interviews with authorities, printed statements by authorities, comments by friends and respected individuals

- **Anecdotes:** personal experiences and the experiences of others, books, television, radio

The reason we ask which sources are the <u>least</u> reliable is the same reason that hearsay is not considered bona fide evidence in a court of law. When people pass along what they <u>think</u> others have said, there are often omissions, additions, and distortions.

Name: _____ Date: _____

Lesson 6: Gathering Information and Using Facts (cont.)

TO THE STUDENT

The largest part of an essay is devoted to facts—details that are selected to show what the writer thinks and why—in order to prove the validity of his or her position. In writing a persuasive essay, you want your readers to at least see that your position is reasonable and thereby to think as you do. You should avoid repeating your opinion without advancing it with supporting evidence. Tie restatements to new pieces of evidence so the reader will have the feeling that you are building your case.

Look again in Lesson 5 at the elements that you decided would strengthen your essay. Where will you get those elements?

1. If you need <u>facts</u> about your topic, where will you get them?

   _____

   _____

   _____

2. If you need <u>examples</u> about your topic, where will you get them?

   _____

   _____

   _____

3. If you need <u>quotations by authorities</u> about your topic, where will you get them?

   _____

   _____

   _____

Name: _____ Date: _____

Lesson 6: Gathering Information and Using Facts (cont.)

4. If you need <u>anecdotes</u> about your topic, where will you get them?

    _____

    _____

    _____

5. For your particular topic, which of the sources you have cited above would be especially useful?

    Facts: _____

    _____

    Examples: _____

    _____

    Quotations: _____

    _____

    Anecdotes: _____

    _____

6. Which is the least reliable of these sources? _____

    Why do you think that? _____

    _____

    _____

    _____

Lesson 7: Organizing the Essay

TO THE TEACHER/PARENT: ABOUT THE LESSON

A simplified analysis of the persuasive essay's organization is given at the beginning of the lesson. Then an example of an essay that sets forth a way of farming is presented. Your students are to delineate the sections of the essay according to whether they are the thesis statement, support for the thesis statement or proposition, or the summarizing statement (conclusion). All of your students should be able to manage this task easily. The lesson ends with some questions about the essay. If taken seriously, they are thought-provoking.

EVALUATING STUDENT RESPONSES

The essay in this lesson is essentially a description of a type of farming, the basis of which is a philosophy about man's relationship with the earth. There are no facts as such presented, and the example given is actually a description of sustainable/organic farming. The writer doesn't really say that using chemicals is harmful to the earth and to humans, but she implies as much. There are no anecdotes or quotations, probably because the writer didn't feel a need for them—presenting a description of her farming method was enough.

Whether this kind of essay would be more effective if buttressed with facts, anecdotes, and quotations is debatable. In assessing your students' responses, the main consideration is the reasons they advance about whether or not the essay is deficient. The argument is found in the description. As an example of the kind of essay that tries to persuade by simply advocating something, it is probably exemplary.

Name: _____ Date: _____

Lesson 7: Organizing the Essay (cont.)

TO THE STUDENT

The way in which a persuasive essay is organized has a lot to do with the impression it makes on the reader. If the essay has a strong, attention-getting beginning, followed by support for the argument that is interesting and logical, it is likely to engage the reader's mind and perhaps emotions.

The **thesis statement**, or **proposition**, at the beginning of a persuasive essay can be regarded as a focusing device. It can offer a solution or make a recommendation.

In the **main body** of the persuasive essay there should be facts, examples, quotations, and anecdotes that **support** the proposition.

An **ending**, or **conclusion**, that sums up the writer's argument will do much to make the essay successful. At the end, the writer can make an emphatic restatement of the proposition or produce a telling bit of evidence to enhance the argument.

The essay that follows can be divided into the parts described above, that is, a beginning with a thesis statement, support for the thesis statement, and a summarizing statement, or conclusion. Put brackets at the beginning and end of each section and label it in the margin.

Rediscovering Farming—Nature's Way

Back to the future. Or perhaps forward to the past. That's the journey upon which sustainable/organic farmers are embarked. Much of today's science is returning to the 1940s and picking up where those farmers left off. Before the birth of chemical agriculture, there was a wealth of knowledge about topics, including hedgerows as habitat, beneficial insects and how to attract them, soil biology, conservation tillage, and more. It is the sustainable/organic farmers' belief that that generation of farmers was right on the cusp of modern organic farming.

These farmers say that research is proving out what has always made sense, namely, that the best way to control disease and insect pests is to have healthy soil, lots of biodiversity and habitat, and not to destroy your soil by excessive rototilling.

Healthy soil has well-defined strata, and tilling it is like putting the biomass in a blender and completely inverting and chopping those layers. Most of the time, a spader is better—it opens and lifts the soil, but puts it

Name: _____ Date: _____

Lesson 7: Organizing the Essay (cont.)

back down without turning it over. Best is the hand hoe, although it is certainly labor-intensive. However, sustainable/organic farmers don't have to go to the gym to stay fit.

Part of the acreage may be planted with a cover crop, which is intended to protect and feed the soil, suppress weeds, and provide habitat for desirable insects. Other sections of the field can have cash crops in varying stages of growth, harvest, or flower. One thing a field will almost never be is fallow. There's a biomass in the soil that needs feeding, and rain will quickly compact bare soil to mud.

The cover crops help to keep down the bane of any farmer's existence: weeds. Every time a weed goes to seed in the field, those seeds can germinate at any time during the following seven years.

Beginning with the first spring planting in late February or early March, and continuing even through the winter months, several crops can be growing at once. The goal is not to have the same family of crops in the same group for at least five years. For example, you can plant the brassica family (broccoli, cauliflower, kale, collards, etc.), and then follow through with legumes, then alliums like onions, leeks, and garlic. It takes about six weeks until a crop is ready to harvest, and then you might fill that area to plant another cash crop or a cover crop, or let what is there go to flower for insectary habitat. The goal is always to have something on the farm blooming for the many insects that are potential predators for things like aphids, root maggots, and cabbage moths.

Sustainable/organic farming is treating the land in an intelligent way that doesn't damage or deplete it. If we are to continue to enjoy bountiful harvests that provide nutritious food, we must pay attention to what these farmers are telling us.

Name: _____ Date: _____

Lesson 7: Organizing the Essay (cont.)

1. "Rediscovering Farming—Nature's Way" does not have all of the elements for an effective persuasive essay that were discussed previously. It describes rather than presents evidence. What elements are missing?

    _____

    _____

    _____

    _____

    _____

2. Would the essay be stronger if it had one or more of those elements? _____

    If so, which ones and why? _____

    _____

    _____

    _____

    _____

    _____

    _____

Lesson 8: Techniques for Conducting an Argument

TO THE TEACHER/PARENT: ABOUT THE LESSON

The rhetorical techniques listed in this lesson are all that are needed in expository persuasive writing. Your students need not be too self-conscious about their use of these techniques; the techniques will come naturally. We only want to point out that there is a wide choice of ways in which to conduct an argument.

EVALUATING STUDENT RESPONSES

This is how we identified the rhetorical techniques that were used in the essay "Mistakes." This particular essay employs about an average number of techniques found in persuasive essays and probably more than are usually found in personal essays.

Mistakes

compare and contrast

define

I'm going to discuss a very unpleasant subject, namely, making mistakes. Of course, there are more disagreeable subjects, such as cancer, civil war, torture, infanticide, famine, and plague, but making goofs, gaffs, and boo-boos reminds us that we are fallible, and most probably foolish, human beings. The depressing part of this failing is that we will always make

discuss

mistakes in all phases of our lives. What can be done about it? Learn from our goofs.

analyze

illustrate

compare and contrast

There are all kinds of mistakes, some terribly serious and some trivial. Interestingly, it's not always the serious mistake that really bugs us. It may be something as inconsequential as repeatedly losing your keys or burning your tongue on a hot dish or drink over and over again. Oftentimes, life-altering mistakes such as deciding not to go to college or quitting an entry-level job aren't the cause of as much consternation as those little mistakes are.

illustrate

discuss

We can profit from our mistakes by determining what went wrong, as scientists do. Scientists actually expect to make mistakes. By altering the conditions of successive experiments, they hope to get nearer to the truth. One of the favorite procedures in science is to formulate a null hypothesis, in which the experimenter states that the expected outcome will be negative.

compare (simile)

summarize

As Will Rogers said, "Good judgment is a matter of experience, and experience is the result of bad judgments." So we must be patient with ourselves and tolerate our goofs in the hope that, like getting lost in an unfamiliar neighborhood, we'll learn something. It may be a little or a lot, but we should try to learn from our mistakes.

Lesson 8: Techniques for Conducting an Argument (cont.)

TO THE STUDENT

Writers employ a variety of rhetorical techniques in setting forth their arguments in a persuasive essay. There are many ways of getting their points across, and it would be a good idea if you reviewed them. You won't want to try to use too many of these techniques in your essay, but you undoubtedly will want to use some of them.

TECHNIQUES FOR SUPPORTING A PROPOSITION

Analyze: to identify main components or aspects; to emphasize special features

Compare: to point out likenesses

Contrast: to point out differences

Define: to explain the meaning of; to distinguish from similar terms

Discuss: to examine in detail

Evaluate: to judge; to give your opinion

Explain: to make clear; to give reasons for

Illustrate: to give one or more examples

Interpret: to give the meaning or significance of

Relate: to tell pertinent stories and anecdotes

Review: to examine on a broad scale

Substantiate: to present facts

Summarize: to examine concisely; to reduce to essentials

Name: _____ Date: _____

Lesson 8: Techniques for Conducting an Argument (cont.)

The following is a persuasive essay that utilizes some of the most effective techniques that can be used in an opinion piece. Read the essay twice. On the second reading, identify the rhetorical techniques that the writer used, and note them in the left-hand margin.

Mistakes

I'm going to discuss a very unpleasant subject, namely, making mistakes. Of course, there are more disagreeable subjects, such as cancer, civil war, torture, infanticide, famine, and plague, but making goofs, gaffs, and boo-boos reminds us that we are fallible, and most probably foolish, human beings. The depressing part of this failing is that we will always make mistakes in all phases of our lives. What can be done about it? Learn from our goofs.

There are all kinds of mistakes, some terribly serious and some trivial. Interestingly, it's not always the serious mistake that really bugs us. It may be something as inconsequential as repeatedly losing your keys or burning your tongue on a hot dish or drink over and over again. Oftentimes, life-altering mistakes such as deciding not to go to college or quitting an entry-level job aren't the cause of as much consternation as those little mistakes are.

We can profit from our mistakes by determining what went wrong, as scientists do. Scientists actually expect to make mistakes. By altering the conditions of successive experiments, they hope to get nearer to the truth. One of the favorite procedures in science is to formulate a null hypothesis, in which the experimenter states that the expected outcome will be negative.

As Will Rogers said, "Good judgment is a matter of experience, and experience is the result of bad judgments." So we must be patient with ourselves and tolerate our goofs in the hope that, like getting lost in an unfamiliar neighborhood, we'll learn something. It may be a little or a lot, but we should try to learn from our mistakes.

Lesson 9: Problems and Pitfalls: Slanted Language

TO THE TEACHER/PARENT: ABOUT THE LESSON

The two tasks of this lesson are to analyze five statements containing slanted language and then to determine whether seven statements may or may not contain slanted language.

Perhaps a discussion of the distinction between a fact and an opinion should precede the administration of the lesson. You can explain that facts are details from experience or observation that can be verified as true. On the other hand, opinions are views of situations based on grounds short of proof. Opinions differ in how they deviate from facts: they can be interpretations, evaluations, or generalizations. An **interpretation** chiefly answers the question, "What does it mean?" An **evaluation** answers questions such as "Is it good?"; "Is it bad?"; "What is it worth?"; and "Is it effective?" **Generalizations** are more complex than the other types of opinions and usually include interpretations and evaluations.

EVALUATING STUDENT RESPONSES

The five statements with slanted language can be analyzed as follows:

1. **FACT:** A.J. Parmalee cast the deciding vote that made the city abandon plans for the park.
   OPINION: The writer identifies A.J. Parmalee as a "notorious naysayer."
   OPINION: The writer calls the action of the city council a "fiasco."
   ANALYSIS: These opinions are incorporated in the statement by using the words "notorious naysayer" and "fiasco," indicating the writer's biased views about the issue.

2. **FACT:** In 1903, the Dawes Commission segregated 1,373,325 acres of Choctaw-Chickasaw land.
   OPINION: The act was "another scandalous maneuver of the U.S. government to deprive the Native Americans of their rights."
   ANALYSIS: The opinion is incorporated in the statement by juxtaposing the fact and the interpretation of it.

3. **FACT:** California's graduation rate is slightly above the national average of 68%.
   OPINION: California's graduation rate is "abysmal."
   ANALYSIS: The writer uses the adjective "abysmal" to describe the graduation rate.

Lesson 9: Problems and Pitfalls: Slanted Language (cont.)

4. **FACT:** The median price of a home in Sonoma County is over $550,000.

   OPINION: Unless more affordable housing is built, 65% of the population will be renters for the rest of their lives.

   ANALYSIS: The writer argues that 65% of the people in Sonoma County will not be able to afford to buy a house unless there is construction of affordable housing (an interpretation and prediction). Although the figure of 65% is given as a fact, that figure is probably an estimate.

5. **FACT:** The artist painted a picture of many trains whistling at once.

   OPINION: The impression on the viewer is "disagreeable."

   ANALYSIS: By applying the adjective "disagreeable" to the noun "impression," the writer (who was reviewing an exhibition of paintings) made a judgment about the painting.

These are analyses of the seven statements at the end of the lesson:

1. Not slanted (NS)
2. Slanted (S)
3. Not slanted (NS)
4. Not slanted (NS)
5. Slanted (S)
6. Slanted (S)
7. Slanted (S)

Name: _____ Date: _____

Lesson 9: Problems and Pitfalls: Slanted Language (cont.)

TO THE STUDENT

Writing that is ostensibly presented in an objective way can include opinions and biased remarks. Most of these slanted messages are not meant to be sneaky or even subtle attempts to influence the reader. They just come naturally to the writer, who has a particular point of view, and thus they intrude themselves in information that appears to be factual. Some writers, however, deliberately insert slanted language into what is supposed to be objective or neutral.

An example will serve to show you how objective reporting can be slanted:

STATEMENT: The Bolivians issued more propaganda this morning about their ridiculous border dispute.

FACT: An announcement was made by Bolivian officials this morning about their border dispute.

OPINION: The writer thinks the announcement was "propaganda."

OPINION: The writer regards the contention made by the Bolivian officials as "ridiculous."

ANALYSIS: The opinion of the writer is hidden in the words "propaganda" and "ridiculous."

Analyze the following statements that contain slanted language.

1. **STATEMENT:** A.J. Parmalee, a notorious naysayer, cast the deciding vote in last night's fiasco at City Hall, forcing the city to abandon plans for the park.

   FACT: _____

   _____

   OPINION: _____

   _____

   OPINION: _____

   _____

   ANALYSIS: _____

   _____

Name: _____ Date: _____

Lesson 9: Problems and Pitfalls: Slanted Language (cont.)

2. **STATEMENT:** In 1903, the Dawes Commission segregated 1,373,325 acres of Choctaw-Chickasaw land—another scandalous maneuver of the U.S. government to deprive the Native Americans of their rights.

   FACT: _____

   _____

   OPINION: _____

   _____

   ANALYSIS: _____

   _____

3. **STATEMENT:** The only comfort California might find in the report is that its abysmal graduation rate is slightly above the national average of 68 percent.

   FACT: _____

   _____

   OPINION: _____

   _____

   ANALYSIS: _____

   _____

Name: _____ Date: _____

Lesson 9: Problems and Pitfalls: Slanted Language (cont.)

4. **STATEMENT:** The median price of a home in Sonoma County is now over $550,000, meaning that 65 percent of the population may be renters for the rest of their lives unless more affordable housing is built.

FACT: _____

_____

_____

_____

OPINION: _____

_____

ANALYSIS: _____

_____

5. **STATEMENT:** The artist tried to give us the disagreeable impression of many trains whistling at once.

FACT: _____

_____

OPINION: _____

_____

ANALYSIS: _____

_____

Name: _____ Date: _____

Lesson 9: Problems and Pitfalls: Slanted Language (cont.)

The following seven statements are comprised of some that have slanted language and some that are only factual. To the left of each statement, indicate whether it is slanted (S) or not slanted (NS). Then explain why it is or isn't guilty of having slanted language.

_____ 1. The West Nile virus kills people, but of the people who are bitten by the carrier mosquito, only one in 150 develops a severe illness.

_____

_____ 2. Construction of the dam actually began secretly in the smoke-filled back room of Jason Long's tavern when the infamous deal was struck, a month before any concrete was poured.

_____

_____ 3. Because of an act of Congress in 1976, credit bureaus must ensure that their records are accurate, and they must give consumers access to their files.

_____

_____ 4. During the 1990s, the wages of the top one-fifth of the workforce increased by 24%, while the bottom one-fifth saw wages increase by 4%.

_____

_____ 5. A Superior Court jury in a questionable decision ruled that the Irvine Medical Center was liable for injuries to Janice Simpson, who suffered respiratory arrest 15 hours after surgery, thus contributing to brain damage.

_____

_____ 6. Scriabin's Second Symphony was played by the Russian Symphonic Society on January 13, 1903, and for thirty or forty minutes, the silence was broken by a continuous series of discords piled up one on top of the other.

_____

_____ 7. Eight million intrepid citizens made their way to the polls, undeterred by threats and harassment.

_____

Lesson 10: Problems and Pitfalls: Emotional Language

TO THE TEACHER/PARENT: ABOUT THE LESSON

This lesson is comprised of a discussion of emotional language, 12 sentences to be analyzed in terms of their emotional content, and a long paragraph that has words that are meant to provoke emotions in the reader. The statements touch upon some sensitive issues, such as abortion, and could therefore trigger emotional reactions from your students. The purpose of the lesson, however, is to warn students that it is easy to get carried away and use emotional language when you feel very strongly about a subject.

EVALUATING STUDENT RESPONSES

These are some interpretations of the 12 statements. There very well could be disagreement with these analyses, proving that language is always capable of ambiguity and misinterpretation and has the capacity, even when expressed in neutral terms, of arousing emotions.

1. In this anecdote, "dilapidated" is perhaps negative, but it ordinarily doesn't provoke much emotion.
2. "Lying scoundrels" is emotive language that in this case was applied to corporate lawyers.
3. "Murder" is the word to trigger emotions, and this word has often been used in arguments about abortion.
4. There is no emotionally charged language in this statement.
5. Nice simile but there is no emotive language.
6. This is a strong statement, but it does not have emotionally charged words, unless "fear" and "insecurity" can be regarded as such.
7. Another strong statement, this sentence was meant to make readers not only think but to arouse emotions in them. It doesn't have words that can be specifically labeled as emotionally charged, but the statement as a whole is emotionally charged. This writer is famous for this kind of approach.
8. This is literally and figuratively strong, emotionally charged language.
9. The entire statement is emotionally charged—and written by a zealot.
10. The word "underhanded" is meant to bring forth emotional responses.
11. "Squalor" is a word with depressing connotations, but this sentence by itself wasn't meant to get the emotions of readers aroused. The writer was trying to appeal to both the intellect and the emotions of her readers in this piece. All in all, however, it is straightforward reporting.
12. There is no specific provocative language in this statement, although "skulking" has negative connotations.

The paragraph contains these pejorative words: "atrocious," "obscene," and "disgustingly greedy."

Name: _____ Date: _____

Lesson 10: Problems and Pitfalls: Emotional Language (cont.)

TO THE STUDENT

In general, there are two ways to appeal to your readers when you write a persuasive essay. The orthodox way is to appeal to their reasoning powers. This is done by presenting a carefully constructed argument, which is also a thorough treatment of the subject. The other approach is to appeal to the readers' emotions. This is often done with language that stirs up passions and prejudices; it may also appeal to the self-interest of the readers. The writers of persuasive essays often appear to be neutral and to present only factual evidence, but they slip emotive language into their essays, sometimes unconsciously. You should avoid injecting emotionally charged words into your persuasive essay, although it may be difficult to avoid doing so.

The following sentences may or may not produce emotions in readers. Read the statements carefully, and then underline those words that definitely have emotional connotations.

1. Charlie climbed into the dilapidated car and made a slight grimace.

2. The lying scoundrels have tried to tell us it was all for our own good.

3. In all cases, this involved the murder of a viable, living embryo.

4. Unlike her graceful older sister, the little girl repeatedly stumbled and whimpered as they scrambled over the rocks.

5. The San Diego County pension fund is like a leaky bucket that can stay full only as long as you've got a hose running into it.

6. I believe it is a combination of fear and insecurity that drives adults to treat teens as they do.

7. Vast numbers of credentialed members of the "caring professions" have a stake in the myth that most people are too fragile to cope with life's vicissitudes and traumas without professional help.

8. The stench from the bottle was comparable to that of having a rabid skunk crawl under your house on a hot summer's day.

9. I don't want my grandchildren exposed to the rantings and ravings of a bunch of '60s-type activists exposing them to radical propaganda.

10. Last March the city acquired 18.5 acres of pasture land in an underhanded deal with a developer who will go unnamed.

11. Nobody should be living in the kind of squalor found at a three-bedroom home raided by state and federal officials last week.

12. He skulked along the littered hallway on his way to a rendezvous with a drug dealer.

Name: _____ Date: _____

Lesson 10: Problems and Pitfalls: Emotional Language (cont.)

The paragraph below is from an essay that has a few emotionally charged words. After you have located the emotional language, rephrase it so that it is neutral and write it on the lines below.

We're Worse Than Selfish

We can't keep on using an atrocious proportion of the world's fossil fuels. It just won't do for Americans to suppose that only their comforts, pleasures, and fancies are important. There are other people on this planet too! As gasoline prices skyrocket and oil corporations reap their obscene profits, we should take heed of these words of Henry Beston: "If there is one thing clear about the centuries dominated by the factory and the wheel, it is that although the machine can make everything from a spoon to a landing-craft, a natural joy in earthly living is something it never has and never will be able to manufacture. It has given us conveniences (often most un-comfortable) and comforts (often most inconvenient), but human happiness was never on its tray of wares. The historical result of the era has been an economic world so glutted with machine power that it is being shaken apart like a jerry-built factory, and a frustrated human world full of neurotic and ugly substitutes for joy." Beston put his finger on the problem—we've been disgust-ingly greedy people who have lost touch with what is important in life.

_____

_____

_____

_____

_____

_____

_____

_____

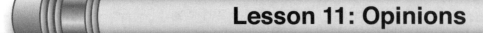
Lesson 11: Opinions

TO THE TEACHER/PARENT: ABOUT THE LESSON

As we state in this lesson, "Opinions," this type of essay doesn't rely on facts and quotations by authorities. Nevertheless, it offers an opinion about fashion that is buttressed with some examples of fashions that can be viewed as frivolous or silly. The writer attempts to show how transitory and mindless fashions can be by citing clothing fashions, both current and long dead, that are ludicrous—at least to him. At the beginning of the essay, he admits his bias in stating that he ordinarily resists any fashion that comes along.

EVALUATING STUDENT RESPONSES

The thesis statement is "Fashion is just plain hokum." The writer uses *examples* to make his case. The elements of "Barely Fashionable" are given in the margin below. In this essay, the examples reinforce the discussion, and otherwise, there is only the force (?) of the writer's argument to persuade the reader.

Barely Fashionable

definition

  Probably the most exasperating thing about fashion is its elusiveness. It's even hard to say what fashion is. Nevertheless, the dictionary gives one definition that suits most of the ways in which we usually use the word fashion: "the current style of dress, conduct, etc." The key word in this definition is "current." The connotations are fairly clear; that is, fashion is a characteristic of something popular in the present, something occurring now. It can also describe something that was popular, of course, as in "yesterday's fashion" or "old-fashioned." Synonyms can range from "style" to

thesis statement

"fad" to "craze." Actually, fashion is just plain hokum.

example

  Fashion as such has always annoyed me. As someone who is temperamentally opposed to being in the majority about almost all trends, I resist fashion. Like other men, I have worn broad ties when they were in style and narrow ones when they were in vogue, but I always felt a little silly and almost hypocritical when I wore either one. Nowadays, men's ties are medium in width, and it has been this way for quite a while, so I no longer feel vaguely uncomfortable when I am forced to put on a tie. I've forgotten

44

Lesson 11: Opinions (cont.)

example

how to tie a Windsor knot, but those swollen wrappings aren't fashionable anymore, and so another uneasy sensation has been eliminated when my wife insists that I put on a tie before draping a suit jacket over my aging shoulders. Nonetheless, if double-breasted suit jackets again become popular and I am nagged into buying such a garment in order to be "in style," I will undoubtedly be uncomfortable. Besides, a man of my girth doesn't cut a very dashing figure in a double-breasted suit.

example

discussion

At the moment, it is fashionable for young women and a few ill-advised, not-so-young women to expose their midriffs in low-slung clothes. That is, the pants or skirt doesn't meet the blouse, T-shirt, or other garment that covers the torso. Scarcely a female from the age of ten to thirty will be seen anywhere in clothes that don't regularly or occasionally reveal a navel and a patch of skin to the south. Some even celebrate the exposure with a tattoo. It's the fashion. Even in winter, when it must prove chilly, a young woman feels compelled to go abroad in clothes that don't cover the middle of her anatomy. How can we explain this strange compulsion? Fashion, everyone says, is the reason. There isn't any reason, I say.

exhortation

Come now, girls—there's nothing unique about an umbilicus. We all have one!

counter-argument

example

The retort of any young person who reads this complaint is that I am old, an unforgivable defect, of course. I can recall that many years ago, the fashion for young people was to have socks that glowed in the dark. (In those days, you could see a boy's ankles.) Now there is a fad that I could tolerate. It even had some practical advantages!

FOLLOWING THROUGH

You might ask your students to write one opinion on a piece of paper, one that can be attacked or supported. These slips should then be placed in a box. Divide the class into groups of three. One member of each group selects a slip from the box, and the group confers to decide how they can make a stand regarding the opinion. The students then work as individuals, writing one paragraph on the topic that has been chosen and using the techniques that they have learned about essay writing.

45

Name: _____ Date: _____

Lesson 11: Opinions (cont.)

TO THE STUDENT

Some persuasive essays can be very much like the personal essay, where the writer expounds upon a subject and makes little or no attempt to back up his or her statement. When the writer builds an argument without marshaling facts and quoting authorities, he or she may be writing a persuasive essay that appeals more to the reader's reasoning faculties. Often essays of this type are found in periodicals. They don't attempt to appeal to the reader's intellect.

That is the case with the essay that follows. Read it first to get the flavor of the piece and a sense of the writer's viewpoint. Then read it again and look for the elements of a persuasive essay and note them in the left-hand margin.

Barely Fashionable

Probably the most exasperating thing about fashion is its elusiveness. It's even hard to say what fashion is. Nevertheless, the dictionary gives one definition that suits most of the ways in which we usually use the word fashion: "the current style of dress, conduct, etc." The key word in this definition is "current." The connotations are fairly clear; that is, fashion is a characteristic of something popular in the present, something occurring now. It can also describe something that was popular, of course, as in "yesterday's fashion" or "old-fashioned." Synonyms can range from "style" to "fad" to "craze." Actually, fashion is just plain hokum.

Fashion as such has always annoyed me. As someone who is temperamentally opposed to being in the majority about almost all trends, I resist fashion. Like other men, I have worn broad ties when they were in style and narrow ones when they were in vogue, but I always felt a little silly and almost hypocritical when I wore either one. Nowadays, men's ties are medium in width, and it has been this way for quite a while, so I no longer feel vaguely uncomfortable when I am forced to put on a tie. I've forgotten how to tie a Windsor knot, but those swollen wrappings aren't fashionable anymore, and so another uneasy sensation has been eliminated when my

Name: _____ Date: _____

Lesson 11: Opinions (cont.)

wife insists that I put on a tie before draping a suit jacket over my aging shoulders. Nonetheless, if double-breasted suit jackets again become popular and I am nagged into buying such a garment in order to be "in style," I will undoubtedly be uncomfortable. Besides, a man of my girth doesn't cut a very dashing figure in a double-breasted suit.

At the moment, it is fashionable for young women and a few ill-advised, not-so-young women to expose their midriffs in low-slung clothes. That is, the pants or skirt doesn't meet the blouse, T-shirt, or other garment that covers the torso. Scarcely a female from the age of ten to thirty will be seen anywhere in clothes that don't regularly or occasionally reveal a navel and a patch of skin to the south. Some even celebrate the exposure with a tattoo. It's the fashion. Even in winter, when it must prove chilly, a young woman feels compelled to go abroad in clothes that don't cover the middle of her anatomy. How can we explain this strange compulsion? Fashion, everyone says, is the reason. There isn't any reason, I say.

Come now, girls—there's nothing unique about an umbilicus. We all have one!

The retort of any young person who reads this complaint is that I am old, an unforgivable defect, of course. I can recall that many years ago, the fashion for young people was to have socks that glowed in the dark. (In those

days, you could see a boy's ankles.) Now there is a fad that I could tolerate. It even had some practical advantages!

Name: _____ Date: _____

Lesson 11: Opinions (cont.)

1. Does the essay have a thesis statement? _____ What is it? _____

_____

_____

_____

2. Upon what element does the essayist principally rely to make his case?

_____

_____

_____

3. What is your response to the writer's argument about fashion?

_____

_____

_____

_____

_____

_____

_____

_____

Lesson 12: Quotes

TO THE TEACHER/PARENT: ABOUT THE LESSON

The quotations in "Napper at Work" add authority, variety, and color to the essay. Although all of the quotations don't strengthen the argument that employees should take naps at work (What about the bosses themselves?), they make the essay easier to read and more interesting. Some students may feel, however, that there are too many quotations in this essay.

EVALUATING STUDENT RESPONSES

This is how we underlined the portions of the essay that raised objections to the proposition that people should take naps on the job. We have also noted the quotations, but they will be readily apparent to your students.

Napper at Work

You're getting sleepy. Very, very sleepy. The computer screen blurs. Your chin bobs southward. The office clock reads 3 P.M. What you wouldn't give for a nap!

Well, take it.

thesis statement — Yeah, go ahead. By most accounts, you'll be a better, more productive worker and a healthier person. And if someone—say your boss—has a problem with it, remind him that our presidents have been known to nap. **examples** — Einstein, in fact, napped, and so did Napoleon.

discussion — Half the world takes a siesta. Napping is an essential biological need, experts say. And as Americans grow ever more sleep-deprived, napping—even at work—has become an acceptable solution. A smattering of U.S. companies have gone so far as to institute employee nap policies. A few have even set up nap rooms for workers. And a fledgling industry of nap promoters is propelling the new attitude.

quote from an authority — "I think there's more awareness of sleep in general and the importance of sleep as one of the pillars of health," says William Anthony, author of "The Art of Napping" and co-author with wife Camille of "The Art of Napping at Work." **indirect quote** — According to Dr. James Maas's 1998 book *Power Sleep*, Americans nap an average of once or twice a week. A quarter of the population never naps, and 30 percent nap more than four times a week. **research facts** — Scientists

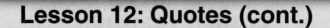

Lesson 12: Quotes (cont.)

say it takes as little as 15 minutes to re-juice our batteries for the next three to four hours.

Still, we're a country in need of some *zzz*s. The average American adult gets six hours and 54 minutes of sleep on weeknights, according to the National Sleep Foundation's 2000 Omnibus Sleep in America poll. A third of adults say they sleep less that 6 1/2 hours a night. Compare that with 1900, when Americans, without electricity, slept an average of 8 1/2 hours at a pop.

quote from an authority

"People erroneously believe they have to burn the midnight oil to succeed," says Dr. Don Weaver, director of the insomnia program at Sleep Medicine Associates of Texas in Dallas. "Their motto is 'The best never rest,' and the truth is, the best rest."

discussion fact

quote from an authority

fact

quote from an authority

Today light bulbs are a comparatively minor distraction. There's 24-hour TV, 24-hour stock trading, and 24-hour WAL-MARTs. Not to mention round-the-clock Internet. (In the National Sleep Foundation poll, 43 percent of adults agreed that they "often stay up later than they should because they are watching TV or are on the Internet.") But even if we did get all the sleep we need at night, we would still experience some inevitable daytime fatigue. "Twice a day, owing to our circadian rhythms," Weaver explains, "our core body temperature reaches its lowest point." It's called the circadian dip, and it occurs around 4 in the morning and 4 in the afternoon." (Note: The latter will happen regardless of whether you've over-indulged at lunch.) "It just so happens that we are maximally sleepy during those times," Weaver says.

discussion

examples

quote

This would pose nary a problem if we were all at home at 4 P.M. with a blanket and no distractions. But most Americans are in no position, literally, for a midday snooze. There are the kids, the boss, the guilt. And, hey, what if you're one of those people who just can't nap? "The few times I've done it, I wake up more tired than I previously was," says Mike Wiles who works for a Cambridge, Massachusetts-based management consulting firm. "It's such a big production, where you have to make sure everything is dark and be sort of warm enough."

Lesson 12: Quotes (cont.)

Wiles's employer even offers him a nap room with a reclining chair (or something like that—the 27-year-old has never actually been in the room). And he does make it a regular New Year's resolution to take naps more often. <u>But, for Wiles, a daytime snooze just doesn't come easily</u>.

discussion

facts

Catching up on sleep isn't simply an act of self-indulgence. The National Sleep Foundation estimates that drowsy workers cost U.S. businesses $18 billion a year in missed workdays and lowered productivity. Fatigued drivers cause 100,000 highway accidents annually.

quote from an authority

facts

"Sleep is just like food, water, and air: It's vital," says Dr. Mark Rosekind, president of Alertness Solutions in Cupertino, California. A sleep researcher for 20 years, Rosekind led a NASA study proving that pilots who were allowed a 40-minute nap during lengthy flights performed better than those who got no shut-eye. Carriers such as British Airways and Qantas Airways have instituted the "NASA nap" as policy.

quote

<u>Corporate types are usually flummoxed by Rosekind's recommendation that they let workers nap. "You want me to pay these people to sleep?" they ask him</u>. "My response is, 'Right now, you're paying them to have their head nod and to drool from 3 to 4 o'clock in the afternoon. What would you spend for a five percent improvement in someone's performance on the job?'"

discussion

<u>Even if business accepted the idea of employee naps, how can Jane Doe, frazzled office manager, relax enough to fall asleep</u>? That's where Tom DeLuca steps in. "The academics say, 'Take a nap!' But that's hard to do," says DeLuca, who bills himself as "the man who's putting corporate America to sleep." His "Power Napping" workshop teaches professionals how to doze amid the chaos and stress of a busy day. "<u>Most people," he</u>

quote from an authority

<u>notes, are "not going to have in their office all those things that they associate with comfort and sleep."</u> DeLuca's technique is part self-hypnosis and part meditation, and all it really requires is comfy head support, a quiet corner, and 15 to 20 minutes.

<u>Nonetheless, DeLuca's clients are shy about going public. When NBC's "Dateline" produced a piece on him this past fall, he had a heck of</u>

Lesson 12: Quotes (cont.)

quote   <u>a time finding a company willing to put its employees to sleep on national</u> <u>television. "There's still a stigma attached to it," he notes.</u>

quote   Not enough of a stigma to deter 55-year-old Art from shutting his office door once a week and snoozing. "It gets to the point where I've got to lie down on the floor," says Art, who declined to give his last name lest his employer find him out. Art banks on the 15-minute power nap, saying it gets him through the rest of his long days. "I'm just doing what I need to do to do what I do at work," he explains.

summarizing statement   Whether or not others can enjoy a nap on the job, you owe it to yourself to try it. I've been napping on the job, with happy results, for years.

There are ten direct quotations in the above essay.

Name: _____ Date: _____

Lesson 12: Quotes (cont.)

TO THE STUDENT

The essay that follows makes a rather convincing case for taking naps on the job, but it also puts forth some commonsense reasons why taking a nap on the job is not practical and is not for everyone. Underline the parts that raise objections to the proposition that people should take naps during working hours.

Notice that the essay contains several quotations by authorities and others. Where there are direct quotations, make notations in the left-hand margin.

Napper at Work

You're getting sleepy. Very, very sleepy. The computer screen blurs. Your chin bobs southward. The office clock reads 3 P.M. What you wouldn't give for a nap!

Well, take it.

Yeah, go ahead. By most accounts, you'll be a better, more productive worker and a healthier person. And if someone—say your boss—has a problem with it, remind him that our presidents have been known to nap. Einstein, in fact, napped, and so did Napoleon.

Half the world takes a siesta. Napping is an essential biological need, experts say. And as Americans grow ever more sleep-deprived, napping—even at work—has become an acceptable solution. A smattering of U.S. companies have gone so far as to institute employee nap policies. A few have even set up nap rooms for workers. And a fledgling industry of nap promoters is propelling the new attitude.

"I think there's more awareness of sleep in general and the importance of sleep as one of the pillars of health," says William Anthony, author of "The Art of Napping" and co-author with wife Camille of "The Art of Napping at Work." According to Dr. James Maas's 1998 book *Power Sleep*, Americans nap an average of once or twice a week. A quarter of the population never naps, and 30 percent nap more than four times a week. Scientists say it takes as little as 15 minutes to re-juice our batteries for the next three to four hours.

Still, we're a country in need of some *zzz*s. The average American adult gets six hours and 54 minutes of sleep on weeknights, according to the National Sleep Foundation's 2000 Omnibus Sleep in America poll. A third of adults say they sleep less that 6 1/2 hours a night. Compare that with 1900, when Americans, without electricity, slept an average of 8 1/2 hours at a pop.

Name: _____ Date: _____

Lesson 12: Quotes (cont.)

"People erroneously believe they have to burn the midnight oil to succeed," says Dr. Don Weaver, director of the insomnia program at Sleep Medicine Associates of Texas in Dallas. "Their motto is 'The best never rest,' and the truth is, the best rest."

Today light bulbs are a comparatively minor distraction. There's 24-hour TV, 24-hour stock trading, and 24-hour WAL-MARTs. Not to mention round-the-clock Internet. (In the National Sleep Foundation poll, 43 percent of adults agreed that they "often stay up later than they should because they are watching TV or are on the Internet.") But even if we did get all the sleep we need at night, we would still experience some inevitable daytime fatigue. "Twice a day, owing to our circadian rhythms," Weaver explains, "our core body temperature reaches its lowest point." It's called the circadian dip, and it occurs around 4 in the morning and 4 in the afternoon." (Note: The latter will happen regardless of whether you've over-indulged at lunch.) "It just so happens that we are maximally sleepy during those times," Weaver says.

This would pose nary a problem if we were all at home at 4 P.M. with a blanket and no distractions. But most Americans are in no position, literally, for a midday snooze. There are the kids, the boss, the guilt. And, hey, what if you're one of those people who just can't nap? "The few times I've done it, I wake up more tired than I previously was," says Mike Wiles who works for a Cambridge, Massachusetts-based management consulting firm. "It's such a big production, where you have to make sure everything is dark and be sort of warm enough."

Wiles's employer even offers him a nap room with a reclining chair (or something like that—the 27-year-old has never actually been in the room). And he does make it a regular New Year's resolution to take naps more often. But, for Wiles, a daytime snooze just doesn't come easily.

Catching up on sleep isn't simply an act of self-indulgence. The National Sleep Foundation estimates that drowsy workers cost U.S. businesses $18 billion a year in missed workdays and lowered productivity. Fatigued drivers cause 100,000 highway accidents annually.

54

Name: _____ Date: _____

Lesson 12: Quotes (cont.)

"Sleep is just like food, water, and air: It's vital," says Dr. Mark Rosekind, president of Alertness Solutions in Cupertino, California. A sleep researcher for 20 years, Rosekind led a NASA study proving that pilots who were allowed a 40-minute nap during lengthy flights performed better than those who got no shut-eye. Carriers such as British Airways and Qantas Airways have instituted the "NASA nap" as policy.

Corporate types are usually flummoxed by Rosekind's recommendation that they let workers nap. "You want me to pay these people to sleep?" they ask him. "My response is, 'Right now, you're paying them to have their head nod and to drool from 3 to 4 o'clock in the afternoon. What would you spend for a five percent improvement in someone's performance on the job?'"

Even if business accepted the idea of employee naps, how can Jane Doe, frazzled office manager, relax enough to fall asleep? That's where Tom DeLuca steps in. "The academics say, 'Take a nap!' But that's hard to do," says DeLuca, who bills himself as "the man who's putting corporate America to sleep." His "Power Napping" workshop teaches professionals how to doze amid the chaos and stress of a busy day. "Most people," he notes, are "not going to have in their office all those things that they associate with comfort and sleep." DeLuca's technique is part self-hypnosis and part meditation, and all it really requires is comfy head support, a quiet corner, and 15 to 20 minutes.

Nonetheless, DeLuca's clients are shy about going public. When NBC's "Dateline" produced a piece on him this past fall, he had a heck of a time finding a company willing to put its employees to sleep on national television. "There's still a stigma attached to it," he notes.

Not enough of a stigma to deter 55-year-old Art from shutting his office door once a week and snoozing. "It gets to the point where I've got to lie down on the floor," says Art, who declined to give his last name lest his employer find him out. Art banks on the 15-minute power nap, saying it gets him through the rest of his long days. "I'm just doing what I need to do to do what I do at work," he explains.

Whether or not others can enjoy a nap on the job, you owe it to yourself to try it. I've been napping on the job, with happy results, for years.

Name: _____ Date: _____

Lesson 12: Quotes (cont.)

1. How many direct quotations are given in the piece? _____

2. Did the quotations strengthen the writer's argument? Why or why not? _____

   _____

   _____

   _____

   _____

   _____

3. The essay does not have a summary statement. Provide it with one here: _____

   _____

   _____

   _____

   _____

   _____

   _____

   _____

   _____

   _____

Lesson 13: Reviews

TO THE TEACHER/PARENT: ABOUT THE LESSON

This lesson isn't about essays as such. It shows the differences between an essay and a review, which often has the look of an essay. Reviews aren't expected to be held to the same standards as are essays. They frequently have emotionally loaded words incorporated in sentences that appear to be factual. Very few reviews, however, are as vitriolic as the one quoted concerning Tchaikovsky's Piano Concerto (written in 1899 in London). George Bernard Shaw wrote some stinging comments about Brahms, Wagner, and others; but he was able to get away with it because of his reputation and the fact that the composers didn't try to sue him.

EVALUATING STUDENT RESPONSES

The first review of Camille Pissarro's "Autumn, Path Through the Woods" has both positive and negative remarks about the painting and the artist. The critic said that "Pissarro has the temperament of a true artist," but he also said that "he is off-and-on; his works bounce from the worst to the best." The sentence about Pissarro's painting freeing itself from the "trappings of its infancy" appears to be a tribute but is really a grudging acknowledgement of Pissarro's talent. In general, the reviewer isn't very sympathetic to Impressionism. ("Pissarro, too has splashed color onto the canvas.")

The second review also has both a positive and a negative flavor. Although the critic seems to praise Pissarro and calls the painting "an impression of great truthfulness, he also states that Pissarro "sometimes approaches the sincerity of Millet," but "does not manage to better the irresolute execution" of Jundt. (What "irresolute execution" means is rather puzzling.) The reviewer says that Pissarro is in the "front rank of the trio of Pissarro, Monet, and Sisley." This statement can be considered an accolade today, since Monet especially is so highly esteemed. The final sentence reveals some reluctance on the critic's part to wholeheartedly accept the Impressionists.

FOLLOWING THROUGH

Ask your students to look in newspapers and magazines for reviews of films, concerts, books, and exhibitions. Most newspapers feature reviews of cultural events, and so each student should be able to find several within a week's time. Have them analyze the reviews, noting biased language but also "fluff pieces" (reviews that are intended to exaggerate the good qualities of an artist or a work). A class discussion of these reviews should be educational and entertaining.

Name: _____ Date: _____

Lesson 13: Reviews (cont.)

TO THE STUDENT

The review of a play, a concert, or an exhibition of paintings is often a kind of essay. The reviewers give their opinions of what they have seen and/or heard. Reviews of plays, films, books, musical performances, and exhibitions of art are rarely impartial and even-handed, however. The reviewers take a position and then support it by giving examples from the works and comparisons with similar works and by measuring the work by some standard of their own choosing. If a review attempts to be objective, it exposes both the faults or weaknesses as well as the strong points of the work.

The review that follows is of a very famous musical composition. The language is emotional, and there is no pretense about its being even-handed about the music or the composer.

Tchaikovsky's Piano Concerto is broken, incoherent, and in at least a dozen instances, the entry of the piano is an impertinent intrusion permitted by the composer because the pianist had to be given something to do. Here is Tchaikovsky, a most "advanced" musician, caring nothing for the rules and forms that served his musical forebears. He wrote a concerto in his earlier days, and, instead of withdrawing it altogether in later life, he revised it! The themes are, without exception, orchestral themes; not one has been thought in the piano idiom. They are simply faked by means of scales and arpeggios to suit the piano.

Interestingly, Tchaikovsky's Piano Concerto is one of the most beloved musical compositions of the past two hundred years.

Next, we have the review of a critic who attempted to be objective about a celebrated painting.

Pissarro has the temperament of a true artist, that is certain. The day that his painting frees itself from the trappings of its infancy, it will be the real modern landscape painting to which the artists of the future will aspire. Unfortunately, the outstanding works in this exhibition are exceptions. Under the pretext of Impressionism, Pissarro, too has splashed color onto canvas. He is off-and on; his works bounce from the worst to the best, like Claude Monet.

Name: _____ Date: _____

Lesson 13: Reviews (cont.)

Was the reviewer impartial, or do you think he had a bias about this kind of art (Impressionism)? Explain.

_____

_____

_____

_____

_____

Here is another review of the same painting.

> Of the trio Pissarro, Monet, and Sisley, Pissarro remains in the front rank. His exhibition is considerable, and it is as interesting as in past years—a singular brotherhood of spirit! Pissarro seems to oscillate between Millet and Jundt. But while he sometimes approaches the sincerity of the former, he does not manage to better the irresolute execution of the latter. I would like to comment on his "Autumn, Path Through the Woods," which creates an impression of great truthfulness. This artist, at least, remains well within the order of sensations that seem to me to be the only plausible justification for Impressionistic art.

Name: _____ Date: _____

Lesson 13: Reviews (cont.)

Was the second reviewer impartial, or did he only give one side? That is, did the review just point out the strong points of the artist and his painting?

_____

Explain why you think this and cite parts of the review to support your contention.

_____

_____

_____

_____

_____

_____

_____

_____

_____

_____

A review is not really an essay, but it may attempt to—and often does—mimic the essay, especially in the critiquing of books, where there may be much more of the writer's thinking than the author's.

Lesson 14: Using Anecdotal Material

TO THE TEACHER/PARENT: ABOUT THE LESSON

This lesson features a short persuasive essay that is well-written but lacks vitality. It is given as an example because it uses all of the elements of a persuasive essay except the one that would make it more interesting, namely, the anecdote. Nonetheless, this essay can be thought of as a thoughtful effort by a competent student writer.

It Has to Be Mutual and Earned

statement of the problem

I am dismayed by the lack of trust all around me. Between young people and old people. Between the police and citizens. Between African-Americans and whites and Hispanics. I am perturbed by the lack of trust throughout the country. Between the Democrats and the Republicans in Congress. Between corporations and unions. Between the public and lawyers. I am appalled by the lack of trust in the world. Between religious groups. Between ethnic groups. Between tribes on three continents. Whenever I pick up a paper and read what is going on, I get very discouraged.

definition

Why is trust important? It is the willingness to believe that the other party will do the right thing by you. Without trust, there can be no satisfactory relationship among people.

proposition

What has caused so much distrust everywhere? I'm not a historian, and so I can't trace the reasons why there has been this growing distrust, but I do see that trust, like respect, must be earned.

1st example

In the family, if children are given opportunities to demonstrate that they are capable of doing the right thing, they can develop and grow because they feel their parents' trust. As Dear Abby said in the famous "Parent's Prayer," "Let me not rob my children of the opportunity to wait on themselves and make decisions." She was talking about trust.

quote

2nd example

When young people get jobs and are given increasing amounts of responsibility, they begin to feel trusted, and they repay their employers with loyalty and conscientiousness.

Lesson 14: Using Anecdotal Material (cont.)

3rd example

In the political sphere, if a leader is backed by the people, even when it isn't clear where he or she is leading them, they will make progress in reaching their goals. Nothing good will happen to an individual or a group of people if there is an absence of mutual trust. It

summarizing statement

must be mutual because trust is a two-way street. The person trusted must also trust.

call to action

Let's show our teachers and administrators that we support them and want to make our schools what they should be. Let's show our police we'll cooperate with them. We know how tough their jobs are. Let's tell our elected officials that we are behind them, and then we can make our community, the country, and the world better. It will take trust on all sides.

EVALUATING STUDENT RESPONSES

It is not obligatory that every persuasive essay have an anecdote. The purpose of this lesson is simply to point out how an anecdote can enhance an essay. Even if your students don't use the anecdotes they write at the end of the lesson, it is a good idea that they at least exercise their memories in relating anecdotes that might work.

Lesson 14: Using Anecdotal Material

TO THE STUDENT

The following is an essay about trust. Read it once to get the idea of the writer's views. Read it again and point out in the left-hand margin the elements (thesis statement or proposition, definition, facts, etc.) that were utilized.

It Has to Be Mutual and Earned

I am dismayed by the lack of trust all around me. Between young people and old people. Between the police and citizens. Between African-Americans and whites and Hispanics. I am perturbed by the lack of trust throughout the country. Between the Democrats and the Republicans in Congress. Between corporations and unions. Between the public and lawyers. I am appalled by the lack of trust in the world. Between religious groups. Between ethnic groups. Between tribes on three continents. Whenever I pick up a paper and read what is going on, I get very discouraged.

Why is trust important? It is the willingness to believe that the other party will do the right thing by you. Without trust, there can be no satisfactory relationship among people.

What has caused so much distrust everywhere? I'm not a historian, and so I can't trace the reasons why there has been this growing distrust, but I do see that trust, like respect, must be earned.

In the family, if children are given opportunities to demonstrate that they are capable of doing the right thing, they can develop and grow because they feel their parents' trust. As Dear Abby said in the famous "Parent's Prayer," "Let me not rob my children of the opportunity to wait on themselves and make decisions." She was talking about trust.

Name: _____ Date: _____

Lesson 14: Using Anecdotal Material (cont.)

When young people get jobs and are given increasing amounts of responsibility, they begin to feel trusted, and they repay their employers with loyalty and conscientiousness.

In the political sphere, if a leader is backed by the people, even when it isn't clear where he or she is leading them, they will make progress in reaching their goals. Nothing good will happen to an individual or a group of people if there is an absence of mutual trust. It must be mutual because trust is a two-way street. The person trusted must also trust.

Let's show our teachers and administrators that we support them and want to make our schools what they should be. Let's show our police we'll cooperate with them. We know how tough their jobs are. Let's tell our elected officials that we are behind them, and then we can make our community, the country, and the world better. It will take trust on all sides.

1. Which element is missing? _____

That's correct, there are no anecdotes. In this particular essay, the writer makes a plea for more trust among people, but this approach could have been enhanced by one or more anecdotes. The relating of personal experiences would have put more life into the essay.

The writer starts off with an impressive listing of situations where trust is woefully lacking. She follows this opening statement of the problem with a definition of trust and then states the proposition (... "trust, like respect, must be earned."). Even with the ensuing example and quotation, the essay doesn't come alive as it would if she had also provided a pertinent anecdote such as the story of the boy sneaking out of his house, which enlivened the essay about rebellion.

Name: _____ Date: _____

Lesson 14: Using Anecdotal Material (cont.)

2. Now think once again about your persuasive essay. Are there any places where your essay can benefit from the inclusion of an anecdote? Think of pertinent experiences of your own and also of people you know. Jot them down below and then see where they can be used effectively in your essay.

_____

_____

_____

_____

_____

_____

_____

_____

_____

_____

_____

_____

_____

Lesson 15: The Other Side

TO THE TEACHER/PARENT: ABOUT THE LESSON

This lesson features a guest editorial that has a form nearly identical to that of the persuasive essay. Effective editorials may or may not have an array of facts, definitions, quotations, examples, or anecdotes, but they all have a thesis statement. This one has several of the elements and techniques of the persuasive essay, and we've asked your students to identify them. In addition, they are to think of points to counter the argument of the writer.

EVALUATING STUDENT RESPONSES

This is how we identified the elements and techniques of the editorial.

Abolish the Color Code!

statement of the problem

technique: discuss and substantiate the example

technique: illustrate

thesis statement

technique: substantiate

quote

As a taxpaying citizen of this community, I've come to the conclusion that enough is enough. The young people of our beloved town are ruining it, and it's the gangs that are doing it! If a young person comes to school wearing a jacket of the wrong color, he may very well be maimed. Look at what happened to that boy in Windsor. He'll be crippled for the rest of his life, and what was the cause of the vicious attack on him? He wore the wrong color of shirt to school. He didn't even belong to a gang. Although it won't solve the problem, the school board at least ought to require that all of our students wear uniforms.

Joseph Thaddeus, the high-priced administrator who was hired last year to be superintendent of the school district, has gone on record as saying he is in favor of uniforms for all of the students in our public schools. (The Catholic school has always had its students wearing uniforms.) The words of Mr. Thaddeus at the last school board meeting are enlightening: "If we don't institute a policy of uniforms for all of our students, the violence will continue. I don't claim that the wearing of uniforms will solve all of these problems with gangs, but it will sure help."

Lesson 15: The Other Side (cont.)

fact

technique: comparing and contrasting

technique: evaluate

restatement of thesis

Santa Anita, our larger neighbor to the north, has already benefited from having a rule of uniforms for all students. As reported in the Santa Anita *Clarion*, the incidences of violence in and around their nine schools has decreased by 85%.

In addition to reducing the incidents of hazing, harassment, and violence in the middle school and senior high school, a strictly enforced policy of uniforms for every student will eliminate the embarrassing garments worn at school by our young women. I'm shocked to see what the girls are allowed to wear in the classroom.

The situation of gang members assaulting each other and intimidating the community can't go on. A first step in eliminating this senseless behavior is to adopt and strenuously enforce a policy of uniforms for all of the students attending our public schools.

Your students may rebut the argument of the writer in a number of ways. These are only a few of the reasons they may offer for opposing the uniform policy:

1. It is undemocratic and dictatorial to force every student to wear the same thing. That's what they did in Nazi Germany.
2. It won't stop gang members from fighting.
3. It is unfair to those students who can't afford to buy the uniform in addition to their regular clothes.
4. Who gets to choose the uniforms? Some students are bound to be unhappy with the choices.
5. The girls are being punished for what the boys do when you force them to wear clothes they don't want to wear.

FOLLOWING THROUGH

You might ask: "Was there any slanted language in the editorial? If so, which words were slanted?"

There is a question as to whether the writer of the editorial is playing upon the fears of the community and is thus attempting to appeal to the emotions of his readers. Ask your students if they believe that he is.

Name: _____ Date: _____

Lesson 15: The Other Side (cont.)

TO THE STUDENT

In preparing a persuasive essay, it is usually a good idea to try to anticipate the points that someone with an opposing viewpoint might have. For example, if you were going to argue that there should be a policy for a school district that all students wear uniforms, you should probably try to think of arguments against such a policy. The following is a guest editorial, which happens to be close to the form of a persuasive essay that advocates just that. The writer of this editorial, however, didn't attempt to counter the arguments of individuals who were opposed to his viewpoint.

Abolish the Color Code!

As a taxpaying citizen of this community, I've come to the conclusion that enough is enough. The young people of our beloved town are ruining it, and it's the gangs that are doing it! If a young person comes to school wearing a jacket of the wrong color, he may very well be maimed. Look at what happened to that boy in Windsor. He'll be crippled for the rest of his life, and what was the cause of the vicious attack on him? He wore the wrong color of shirt to school. He didn't even belong to a gang. Although it won't solve the problem, the school board at least ought to require that all of our students wear uniforms.

Joseph Thaddeus, the high-priced administrator who was hired last year to be superintendent of the school district, has gone on record as saying he is in favor of uniforms for all of the students in our public schools. (The Catholic school has always had its students wearing uniforms.) The words of Mr. Thaddeus at the last school board meeting are enlightening: "If we don't institute a policy of uniforms for all of our students, the violence will continue. I don't claim that the wearing of uniforms will solve all of these problems with gangs, but it will sure help."

Name: _____ Date: _____

Lesson 15: The Other Side (cont.)

Santa Anita, our larger neighbor to the north, has already benefited from having a rule of uniforms for all students. As reported in the Santa Anita *Clarion*, the incidences of violence in and around their nine schools has decreased by 85%.

In addition to reducing the incidents of hazing, harassment, and violence in the middle school and senior high school, a strictly enforced policy of uniforms for every student will eliminate the embarrassing garments worn at school by our young women. I'm shocked to see what the girls are allowed to wear in the classroom.

The situation of gang members assaulting each other and intimidating the community can't go on. A first step in eliminating this senseless behavior is to adopt and strenuously enforce a policy of uniforms for all of the students attending our public schools.

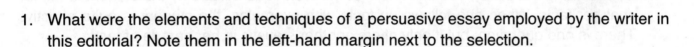

1. What were the elements and techniques of a persuasive essay employed by the writer in this editorial? Note them in the left-hand margin next to the selection.

2. What are some of the points that could be raised in opposition by someone with a contrary viewpoint? List them below.

_____

_____

_____

_____

_____

Lesson 16: Reviewing the Elements of a Persuasive Essay

TO THE TEACHER/PARENT: ABOUT THE LESSON

The essay held up for critical reviewing in this lesson was probably considered excellent by the student's teacher. As an essay that sets out to make an argument by amassing facts, it is admirable. It also has a personal touch that helps younger readers identify with the writer. Nonetheless, for our purposes of instructing your students in regard to writing a persuasive essay, it is not complete, and its logic is faulty. We don't want to be picky, however, and it must be admitted that the student "did her homework (research)."

EVALUATING STUDENT RESPONSES

The following are the points that concern us about the essay. If your students disagree about our contentions, so much the better. However, given the precepts that have been presented in the first few lessons of this book, the essay is deficient.

1. The presentation of facts and examples to back up the student's argument about the standards of literacy in this country is commendable. Those facts and examples are the strength of her argument.
2. The student's essay omits these elements: definitions, consideration of counter-arguments, true anecdotes, and comparisons.
3. Her thesis statement comes in the third paragraph: "Apparently one of my favorite activities is not one at which most Americans are proficient when it comes to higher-level reading." This is a sweeping generalization.
4. By analyzing the essay, you can see that the technique utilized by the student is to marshal her facts. When she follows up facts with examples, the student is quite effective. There is one quotation, but it only offers another statistic in her parade of facts.
5. Because of their dominance, the statistics tend to be boring.
6. The opening is a plus. She makes it personal, which helps mitigate the surfeit of facts that follows.
7. She doesn't define "higher-level reading." What *is* higher-level reading?
8. The weakest part of the student's argument is her logical thinking. As she says, no one is expected to read the doctor's handwriting, and the only writing on the prescription labels that she says we should read is the dosage. That would seem to be crucial, of course; but she is on shaky ground in citing the problems people have with their Medicare applications. That isn't so much a matter of reading proficiently as it is of writing understandably.
9. The problem, apparently, is not a matter of technically defining "literate." It is of poor, semi-literate readers!
10. All in all, when read thoughtfully, the essay makes some kind of sense. On the other hand, it doesn't have enough force, and she doesn't have suggestions about how to alleviate the problem.

Lesson 16: Reviewing the Elements of a Persuasive Essay (cont.)

TO THE STUDENT

The following is an essay by a 16-year-old girl about literacy in the United States. Read it carefully twice, and then answer the questions below.

Re-examining the Definition of "Literate"

Sitting up late at night in bed, I listen carefully for any sound that my mom is approaching my room. If she notices that my lights are on, she will come in and force me to go to sleep. You might ask, what am I doing up at that time of night?

The answer: reading.

Apparently one of my favorite activities is not one at which most Americans are proficient when it comes to higher-level reading.

The CIA World Factbook states that 97 percent of our population is literate, meaning those over the age of 15 can read and write. Yet that does not take into account the disparate levels of ability.

According to a survey done by the National Center for Education Statistics, in the 1990s more than 100 million of about 191 million adults demonstrated skills in the lowest two of the five literacy levels.

The 21 to 23 percent in Level 1 and the 25 to 28 percent in Level 2 ranged in ability from being unable to respond to much of the survey, to having difficulty making low-level connections with simple word problems, such as the difference in price between two items, and even finding an intersection on a street map.

They could not respond correctly to problems involving high-level reading or problem-solving skills. However, 66 to 75 percent in Level 1 and 93 to 97 percent in Level 2 identified themselves as reading or writing English "well" or "very well."

Almost 33 percent of the people were in Level 3 and could solve problems involving multiple arithmetic operations when they set up the problem on their own.

Only 18 to 21 percent, less than 40 million adults, were assessed as being in Level 4 or 5. They had proficiency comprehending long and complex documents and passages.

According to the National Assessment of Adult Literacy, "... nearly half of all adults in the lowest level on each literacy scale were living in poverty, compared with only 4 to 8 percent of those in the two highest proficiency levels."

Lesson 16: Reviewing the Elements of a Persuasive Essay (cont.)

The Literacy Information and Communication Systems (LINCS) affirms the 1997 statistics that 62 percent of children under the age of six with parents that had less than a high-school education were under the poverty level, compared to nearly 3 percent among children whose better-educated parent has a college degree.

A 1993 study of 3,659 hospital patients reported that over 23 percent of patients surveyed had inadequate health literacy and did not know how to take their medicine.

Only 4.5 percent of the patients in that study had adequate health literacy. Most patients, up to 81 percent, were unable to comprehend their Medicare applications.

We must improve our country's literacy levels, especially when people have difficulty understanding their own prescriptions.

It is bad enough trying to decipher doctors' handwriting without the added difficulty of not being literate enough to understand the basics of medicine dosages.

When 97 percent of our population is considered literate, why do so many still have difficulties understanding prescriptions or reading maps?

Maybe we need to change our definition of "literate."

1. The student has obviously done a good deal of research for this essay. Is her argument more convincing because of her preparation? _____

   Explain why or why not. _____

   _____

   _____

   _____

2. Does the student have enough elements in her essay (facts, examples, quotes, anecdotes, etc.)? _____

   If not, which ones has she left out? _____

   _____

   _____

Name: _____ Date: _____

Lesson 16: Reviewing the Elements of a Persuasive Essay (cont.)

3. If there is a thesis statement, what is it? _____

_____

4. What is her main technique in arguing her case? _____

_____

5. Does the student have *too many* facts in her essay? _____

Explain. _____

_____

6. Do you like the opening? _____ Why or why not? _____

_____

_____

7. Would her essay have been more convincing if she had defined any of the terms in it?

_____ If so, which terms need defining? _____

_____

8. Is the student's reasoning suspect at any point? _____ For example, she states:

"We must improve our country's literacy levels, especially when people have difficulty un-

derstanding their own prescriptions."

9. Is the problem that "we need to change our definition of literate"? _____

Explain. _____

_____

10. Were you persuaded by the student's argument? _____ Why or why not?

_____

_____

_____

Lesson 17: Writing Your Persuasive Essay

TO THE TEACHER/PARENT: ABOUT THE LESSON

The last lesson has your students writing their persuasive essays. After having analyzed many essays that have used the elements of and techniques for writing a persuasive essay, they finally get to write one. It may be an anticlimax for those students who could have written a good persuasive essay long before (or so they believe).

We offer a checklist so that your students can have something to guide them as they prepare to write their first drafts.

It is recommended that your students submit their second drafts to a different student for critiquing; theoretically, they will have a relatively convincing essay after having gone through the many steps that have been specified. If they have been conscientious in following the steps, you may have a batch of excellent essays to review.

EVALUATING STUDENT RESPONSES

Even though your students incorporate all of the elements into their essays, use many of the rhetorical techniques, and avoid the pitfalls of slanted and emotional language, their essays may not be satisfactory because their logic is faulty. Unfortunately, you won't be able to rely on students to detect these defects. It's a job for the teacher.

Some of the common problems in logical thinking that you may encounter are these:
- Ambiguous language
- Vague language
- Logical fallacies
- Stereotyping
- Non sequiturs
- Begging the question
- Either/or fallacy (when two positions are falsely presented as the only alternatives)
- Emotional fallacies
    - Ad hominem (attacking the man rather than his position on the issue)
    - Ad populum (appealing to prejudices and fears)
    - Name calling
    - Glittering generality
    - Bandwagon appeal

Your students are more likely to use slanted or emotional language than to employ logical fallacies in their essays. Nevertheless, one or more of those errors might creep into their writing.

Name: _____ Date: _____

Lesson 17: Writing Your Persuasive Essay (cont.)

TO THE STUDENT

Now that you have studied the elements of a persuasive essay and learned about the techniques of writing one, it is time to gather up your outline and all your preparatory notes and put them together in a first draft on your own paper. The important thing is to write the essay. It won't be perfect, of course, because it's just the first draft.

To review what has been stated several times in previous lessons, the basis for a persuasive essay is a reasonable opinion and plenty of specific evidence for it. You have been urged to keep your readers in mind as you write your essay. We also have recommended that you have a fellow student read it critically after you have written a first draft. (See Lesson 1.)

The value of having someone critique your work is rather obvious. First of all, the writer knows what he or she is trying to say, and so some words may not get written down because they are assumed by the writer. In contrast, the reader must depend entirely on the words and how they are expressed in order to understand the argument. Secondly, the reader brings to a reading of the essay different perceptions than those of the writer. In addition, oftentimes the reader has different values. Accordingly, if the writer is to be successful in making a persuasive argument, he or she must keep in mind who will read the essay. The quickest way to get feedback about the effectiveness of your essay, then, is to have a fellow student read it.

Use the following checklist to make sure you have done an adequate job of writing your persuasive essay before giving it to a fellow student to read.

CHECKLIST AFTER YOUR FIRST DRAFT

When you have finished your essay, you should ask yourself a few questions.

1. Did I make a thesis statement in the beginning?

2. Have I defined important terms?

3. Do I have facts, examples, anecdotes, and/or quotations to support my opinion? The evidence you give is the most important part of your essay.

4. Did I avoid the use of broad generalizations instead of presenting facts? Generalizations of widely accepted ideas are more effective than generalizations that rest upon vague assumptions.

5. Did I organize my facts, examples, and anecdotes in such a way as to present a persuasive argument?

6. Did I demonstrate that I had a clear idea of what I wanted to say?

7. Did I make an emphatic restatement of my argument at the end of the essay?

Name: _____ Date: _____

Persuasive Essay Writing Assessment

To determine how much you have learned about persuasive essay writing, revisit the short essay you wrote when you began this unit in which you tried to persuade younger students to eat a balanced diet in order to maintain a healthy lifestyle. Using what you now know about persuasive writing, is there anything you would change? Do you think you could do a better job on the essay now? Well, here's your chance. Rewrite the essay using what you have learned in this unit. The essay should be as long as necessary to convey your message, but it must be at least three paragraphs long. Use your own paper if you need more room.

_____

_____

_____

_____

_____

_____

_____

_____

_____

_____

_____

_____

_____

_____

Persuasive Essay Writing Assessment (cont.)

_____

_____

_____

_____

_____

_____

_____

_____

_____

_____

_____

_____

_____

_____

_____

_____

_____

_____

_____

_____

_____

_____

Sample Topics for Persuasive Essays

- Adoption
- After School Jobs
- Alternative Fuels/Energy Sources
- Art Appreciation
- Beauty Pageants
- Cancer Research
- Careers
- Classical Music
- College/Higher Education
- Community Watch Groups
- Computer Literacy
- Country Music
- Curfews
- Disaster Preparedness
- Dress Codes
- Driving Age
- Drug Abuse
- Exercise
- Extracurricular Activities
- Family Reunions
- Family Vacations
- Foreign Exchange Programs
- Gambling
- Healthy Eating
- Homelessness
- Internet Chat Rooms
- Local Issues
- Low-income Housing
- Nuclear Power
- Performance of Political Leaders
- Poverty
- Product Safety

- Public Transportation
- Race Relations
- Rap Music
- Reading
- Reality TV Shows
- Smoking
- Space Exploration
- Speed Limits
- Sports
- Taking Foreign Language Classes
- Teen Drinking
- Teen Employment
- Teen Pregnancy
- Teen Suicide
- The Health Care System
- The Minimum Wage
- Using Child Safety Seats
- Vehicle Safety
- Volunteering
- Voting Age
- Wearing Seat Belts
- World Travel